It's Snow!

Elisa Peters

PowerKiDS press™

New York

For Morgan Downer

Published in 2009 by The Rosen Publishing Group, Inc.
29 East 21st Street, New York, NY 10010

First Edition

Editor: Amelie von Zumbusch
Book Design: Greg Tucker
Photo Researcher: Jessica Gerweck

Photo Credits: Cover, back cover images, pp. 5, 7, 11, 13, 15, 17, 19, 21, 23 by Shutterstock.com; p. 9 by NOAA.

Library of Congress Cataloging-in-Publication Data

Peters, Elisa.
  It's snow! / Elisa Peters. — 1st ed.
      p. cm. — (Everyday wonders)
  Includes index.
  ISBN 978-1-4042-4462-7 (library binding)
  1. Snow—Juvenile literature. I. Title. II. Series.
  QC926.37.P48 2009
  551.57'84—dc22

                                                    2007046449

Manufactured in the United States of America

Contents

It is fun to play in the snow!

Snow is white.

Snow is made up of many little **snowflakes**.

Snowflakes fall from the sky.

When snow falls, it covers everything.

Animals, like this **squirrel**, have to dig in the snow to find food.

Snow is fun. You can go **sledding** in the snow.

You can make a **snow angel**.

You can build a snowman, too.

Making a snow house is another fun thing to do in the snow.

Words to Know

sledding

snow angel

snowflake

squirrel

Index

Web Sites

Due to the changing nature of Internet links, PowerKids Press has developed an online list of Web sites related to the subject of this book. This site is updated regularly. Please use this link to access the list:
www.powerkidslinks.com/wonder/snow/